US ARMED FORCES

# JOIN THE MARINES

HOT TOPICS

By P. P. Mitchell

Gareth Stevens Publishing

**Please visit our website, www.garethstevens.com. For a free color catalog of all our high-quality books, call toll free 1-800-542-2595 or fax 1-877-542-2596.**

Library of Congress Cataloging-in-Publication Data

Names: Mitchell, P. P., author.
Title: Join the Marines / P. P. Mitchell.
Description: New York : Gareth Stevens Publishing, [2018] | Series: US Armed Forces | Includes index.
Identifiers: LCCN 2017000304| ISBN 9781538205440 (pbk. book) | ISBN 9781538205457 (6 pack) | ISBN 9781538205464 (library bound book)
Subjects: LCSH: United States. Marine Corps--Juvenile literature. | United States. Marine Corps--Vocational guidance--Juvenile literature.
Classification: LCC VE23 .M55 2018 | DDC 359.9/602373--dc23
LC record available at https://lccn.loc.gov/2017000304

Published in 2018 by
**Gareth Stevens Publishing**
111 East 14th Street, Suite 349
New York, NY 10003



Designer: Bethany Perl
Editor: Joan Stoltman

Photo credits: Cover, 1-32 (camouflage) Casper1774 Studio/Shutterstock.com; cover, pp. 1-32 (grunge effect) iulias/Shutterstock.com; cover, pp. 1-32 (rounded text box) foxie/Shutterstock.com; cover, pp. 1-31 (border) jumpingsack/Shutterstock.com; pp. 2-32 (text box) Olga_C/ Shutterstock.com; p. 5 Leonard Zhukovsky/Shutterstock.com; pp. 5-29 (dog tag) Feng Yu/ Shutterstock.com; photos courtesy of US Marine Corps: cover, p. 1 by Sgt. Jacob Harrer, p. 5, 7 by Lance Cpl. Jason Morrison, p. 9 by Gunnery Sgt. Rome M. Lazarus, p. 11 by Lance Cpl. Zachery C. Laning, p. 13 Cpl. Marionne T. Mangrum, p. 15 by Lance Cpl. Andrew Kuppers, p. 17 by Lance Cpl. Dan Hosack, p. 19 by Lance Cpl. Jose Villalobosrocha, p. 21 by Cpl. Elize McKelvey, p. 23 by Sgt. Jamean Berry, p 27 by Chief Warrant Officer 2 Paul S. Mancuso, p. 29 by Lance Cpl. Angelica I. Annastas; p. 17 (American Flag) Nataliia K/Shutterstock.com; p. 25 TJ Brown/Shutterstock.com; p. 30 (snow MARPAT) Lance Corporal Sarah Anderson/Wikipedia.com; p. 30 (desert MARPAT) Sgt. Luis R. Agostini/Wikipedia.org; p. 30 (woodland MARPAT) Lance Cpl. Juan D. Alfonso/ Wikipedia.org.



Printed in the United States of America

CPSIA compliance information: Batch #CS17GS: For further information contact Gareth Stevens, New York, New York at 1-800-542-2595.

# CONTENTS

# ALL ABOUT THE MARINE CORPS!

Marines are some of the top fighters in the armed forces! Marines train for all kinds of **missions** in water, on land, and in the air. Their training is really hard, so being a marine isn't meant for everyone.

## DID YOU KNOW?

There are only around 180,000 active marines, one-third the number of soldiers in the army!

Marines are able to change quickly. They are stationed, or live and work, all over the world, so that they can move quickly to wherever they're needed. A big part of their mission is to be the first on the scene.

## DID YOU KNOW?

Before marines are sent somewhere new, they learn about the local language, **culture**, history, land, weather, and more!

All marines are trained to be leaders in case they need to make quick decisions during a **crisis**. Every marine is a rifleman, which means they're trained to shoot and fight well, even if they're not **assigned** to a fighting job!

## DID YOU KNOW?

*Ductus exemplo*, which is Latin for "lead by example," is a saying used a lot in the marines!

# HOW DO I JOIN?

There are two ways to enter the marines: sign up to join as an enlisted marine, or become an officer. They both lead and work on the same missions, but enlisted marines and officers train to do different jobs within each mission.

## DID YOU KNOW?

Enlisted marines make up most of the marine corps. However, there are several programs that can train enlisted marines to become officers.

You can enlist at age 18 by talking with a recruiter, or a person in your community who helps people join the armed forces. Then, you'll take a test that shows your strengths and matches you to a job in the marines.

**DID YOU KNOW?**

A rank is a title that shows your responsibility, or duty, in the armed forces. The higher the rank, the more pay, responsibility, and skill a person has earned.

Next, you'll take a physical test, which includes pull-ups or **flexed**-arm hangs and a swimming test. After passing both, you're off to basic training camp! All marines take two physical tests every year to make sure they're staying in shape.

## DID YOU KNOW?

You'll also train constantly to get better at your job, rise in the ranks, and stay prepared to move quickly in new missions.

To become an officer, you must finish a 4-year college. You can start training for your commissioning during college. An Officer Selection Officer, or OSO, will help you decide your path.

**DID YOU KNOW?**

When you're commissioned, this means you've officially become an officer.

# OFFICER MARINE RANKS

GENERAL

LIEUTENANT GENERAL

MAJOR GENERAL

BRIGADIER GENERAL

COLONEL

LIEUTENANT COLONEL

MAJOR

CAPTAIN

FIRST LIEUTENANT

SECOND LIEUTENANT

You have to pass training at the marines' officer candidate school (OCS) to become an officer. Most people finish OCS by taking the platoon leader-training course in summers during college. You can also take the officer candidate course after college.

**DID YOU KNOW?**

Officer jobs are broken down into three groups: ground jobs, air jobs, and law jobs.

# WHAT JOB COULD I HAVE?

There are many jobs to do in the marines, such as fixing weapons, keeping **communication** systems running, inventing tools, and keeping track of money and supplies. Marines can be **engineers**, practice law, or even fly planes!

## DID YOU KNOW?

A job in the US armed forces is called a military occupational specialty (MOS). MOSs are assigned based on what you'd like to do, what you're good at, and what your branch of the armed forces needs.

Marines guard over 100 United States **embassies** throughout the world. Thousands of marines are deployed, or sent to work, on ships along the world's coasts so they can respond quickly if something happens!

**DID YOU KNOW?**

There are 12 marine bases in the United States, and one in Japan.

# MARINES AND THE PRESIDENT

Four specially trained marine pilots, nicknamed "The Nighthawks," fly the president in a helicopter called Marine One. Marines also guard the president whenever the president is at the White House or addressing the press outside in the Rose Garden.

## DID YOU KNOW?

Marine One can fly over 150 miles (240 km) per hour to get the president to safety quickly. It has armor to keep everyone inside safe.

# THE UNIFORM

The marine corps has three different patterns of **camouflage** for their combat, or battle, uniforms. They're also called field uniforms, utilities, cammies, or MCCUU (marine corps combat utility uniforms). The camouflage patterns are called MARPAT, short for marine pattern.

## DID YOU KNOW?

MARPAT has only been used by the marines since 2002! It's a pattern made on a computer, which works much better than other patterns. MARPAT was the first digital pattern used by any branch of the US armed forces.

# HOW CAN I GET READY NOW?

You can get ready for the marines now! It's important that you start exercising and learning how to keep your body healthy and in shape. Also, seek out leadership positions on sports teams, in clubs, and in your classroom.

## DID YOU KNOW?

Future marines need to practice listening to others, thinking through decisions, and thinking before they speak and act.

# MARINE CAMOUFLAGE

# FOR MORE INFORMATION

## Books

Berne, Emma Carlson. *Today's U.S. Marines*. North Mankato, MN: Compass Point Books, 2013.

Miller, Adam. *U.S. Marines True Stories: Tales of Bravery*. North Mankato, MN: Capstone Press, 2015.

Raum, Elizabeth. *U.S. Marines by the Numbers*. North Mankato, MN: Capstone Press, 2014.

## Websites

**Exhibits: National Museum of the Marine Corps**
*usmcmuseum.com/exhibits.html*
Read all about what the US Marine Corps Museum in Virginia has to offer!

**US Marine Corps**
*marines.com/home*
Check out the US Marines website!

**Publisher's note to educators and parents:** Our editors have carefully reviewed these websites to ensure that they are suitable for students. Many websites change frequently, however, and we cannot guarantee that a site's future contents will continue to meet our high standards of quality and educational value. Be advised that students should be closely supervised whenever they access the Internet.

# GLOSSARY

**assign:** to give someone a certain job or duty

**camouflage:** colors or shapes on clothing that allow people to blend in with their surroundings

**communication:** the ways of sending information to people

**crisis:** a hard or unsafe situation that needs serious attention

**culture:** the beliefs and ways of life of a group of people

**embassy:** the home and office building of an ambassador, a politician who acts for his or her own government while living in another country

**engineer:** a person who uses science and math to build better objects

**flexed:** bent

**mission:** a task or job a group must carry out

# INDEX